Press of
Back Pages Publishers

Waltham, MA

Engravings by Max G. Widmauer

FACTORY OF THE AMERICAN WALTHAM WATCH COMPANY

A MODEL FACTORY
IN A MODEL CITY:

A SOCIAL STUDY.

BY

JOHN SWINTON

WITH AN
INTRODUCTION
BY

LAURENCE A. GREEN

1887.

JOHN SWINTON'S PAPER:

AN INTRODUCTION*

Published in 1887, "A Model Factory in a Model City" presents a short, detailed account of a week in the life of the employees and directors of the Waltham Watch Factory. It is not known if or where it was sold. It is not known if its author, John Swinton had an academic reason for writing it — as his subtitle "A Social Study" suggests — or if he was paid by the company to do so. Whatever his original intent the style in which this uncommon glimpse into the past is written carries the silly, slightly pompous, and overly effusive tone that propaganda often acquires when its immediate use and purpose have passed.

That the model factory featured in his booklet was the exceptionally innovative Waltham Watch Company makes "A Model Factory in a Model City" particularly compelling. It is of equal importance that the model city was Waltham, Massachusetts, the birthplace of the American Industrial Revolution. But it is the narrator who makes this sketch of labor conditions in the late 19th century at once so valuable and so odd. How is it that a pamphlet praising the owners of one of the largest specialized factories in the world at that time came to be written by John Swinton, among the most prominent radical socialist writers in American history?

In 1887, Swinton was one of the foremost journalists on the continent. Born in Scotland, he traveled to Canada before moving to the United States in the mid-1840's. He worked as a printer and journalist, briefly passing through the Williston Seminary in Massachusetts in 1853.[i] An ardent abolitionist, he followed the steady escalation of tension between the northern and southern states with keen interest. When violence over slavery reached a boiling point in the mid-1850's, Swinton abruptly packed his bags and headed south to work as a newspaperman in Lawrence, Kansas, one of the most unstable territories in America.[ii]

In 1857 he returned to the north to study medicine and law in New York City. After submitting a number of articles to *The New York Times* he was appointed their managing editor and remained in that position from 1860 until the close of the decade. He then moved to *The New York Sun*, where he was an editorial writer for over twenty years.[iii]

Living through draft riots, race riots, and profiteering in New York during the war, Swinton bore witness to horrific degradation and cruelty. What he observed solidified his belief that slavery was the extension of a greater class war perpetrated by the wealthy against the poor.[iv] After the assassination of Abraham Lincoln, he grew increasingly ardent, outraged at the exponential growth of American industry and the attendant exploitation of the poor and working classes in pursuit of huge profits. His views simultaneously turned inward; he increasingly came to believe that the media was guilty for publicly extolling what he thought to be non-existent virtues of post-war American industry.[v]

In the waning decades of the century, New York tenements became a haven for thousands of immigrants who were frequently exploited and shepherded into wage slavery across the nation.[vi] Landscapes of poverty and abuse, these neighborhoods became an object of outrage for Swinton. Presaging a generation of social-reform journalists like Upton Sinclair and Lewis Hine, Swinton sought out slave-traders and wrote investigative works detailing the ways in which they lured immigrants into indentured servitude in shoe factories, cigar factories and steel mills.[vii] His politics radicalized as strikes broke out in cities, mill towns, and mining camps across the country. He began giving public speeches on behalf of workers' rights.[viii] The largest industrial labor movement in American history had erupted. Workers demanded equal pay, equal representation, and reasonable hours. They demanded safe working conditions and an end to child labor. At the forefront of it all, in print and in person, was John Swinton.

With his influence from *The Sun*, Swinton traversed union halls, rallies, strikes, pubs, dives, and hangouts.[ix] He befriended anarchist leaders, budding socialists, radical poets, and foreign philosophers. He conversed regularly with Emma Goldman, exchanged letters with Walt Whitman, hosted the prominent anarchocommunist Peter Kropotkin in New York, mentored the young socialist Eugene V. Debs, and interviewed Karl Marx.[x]

Asked to speak at the New York Press club in 1884 about the state of the independent press, Swinton launched into his most famous screed, refracting his view of America through his beliefs about media and industry:

> "There is no such thing, at this stage of the world's history in America, as an independent press. You know it and I know it. There is not one of you who dare write your honest opinions, and if you did, you know beforehand that it would never appear in print. I am paid weekly for keeping my honest opinions out of the paper I am connected with. Others of you are paid similar salaries for similar things, and any of you who would be foolish as to write honest opinions would be out on the streets looking for another

job. If I allowed my honest opinions to appear in one issue of my papers, before twenty-four hours my occupation would be gone. The business of the journalist is to destroy the truth, to lie outright, to pervert, to vilify, to fawn at the feet of Mammon, and to sell his country and his race for his daily bread. You know it and I know it, and what folly is this toasting an independent press? We are the jumping jacks, they pull the strings and we dance. Our talents, our possibilities and our lives are all the property of other men. We are intellectual prostitutes."[xi]

Swinton had observed decades of unquestionable decline—the coalescing of corporate and media power at the expense of the poor—but in Waltham such a decline was not entirely evident. Around the time he was studying at Williston Seminary, the Selectmen of Waltham were deciding whether or not to purchase 600 acres of land from the neighboring town of Newton so that the industrial quarter of the town could span both sides of the river.[xii] Throughout the 18th century, Waltham had grown from a rural village into a semi-commercial hamlet with a handful of paper mills.[xiii] At the outset of the 1800's, the town had become home to the summer estates of some of Boston's wealthiest citizens and in 1811 Francis Cabot Lowell arrived with plans to open the first fully industrialized factory in North America.[xiv]

Lowell organized a group of investors and together they formed a corporation that raised $100,000 to build the Boston Manufacturing Company.[xv] They hired young women from surrounding farms, and opened at a particularly fortuitous moment. Reeling from the War of 1812, the nascent American economy demanded a stable supply of basic goods that would allow the emerging domestic business environment to circumvent the vulnerabilities inherent in shipping to and from foreign markets. Lowell's mill was able to take raw cotton and turn it into cloth without any additional labor needed to complete the process, all while lessening extreme dependence on international trade.[xvi] It was an almost immediate financial success. The partners expanded their operations to meet demand but, after a meteoric inception, six years into their experiment Francis Cabot Lowell succumbed to chronic illness and died.[xvii]

It was a stunning loss but Lowell left behind a meticulously organized system and the partners regrouped without their leader. In 1820, the company built its third mill and with it they reached the maximum manufacturing capacity of the Charles River in Waltham.[xviii] Looking across the region they directed their attention toward the small village of East Chelmsford. In 1823 they incorporated the first factory town in American history and renamed East Chelmsford in honor of their departed founding partner.[xix]

The mill in Waltham continued to produce cloth and was successful, but the verve of the industrial revolution moved along, leaving a diverse set of farms and local businesses to coexist with the factory. Many of the abuses that almost immediately came to distinguish life in the expanding network of New England mill towns also passed by Waltham and though the population increased, the town remained comparatively small.[xx]

In 1849, the Selectmen decided to purchase the land from Newton.[xxi] The demand to house new industries in the town was great, and space was needed to accommodate them, but across New England two rapid declines—one social and the other comprehensively financial—were set to befall the region. Just as large numbers of New Englanders were giving up their farms and moving to the mill towns and cities, Irish immigrants began arriving in unprecedented numbers, fleeing the Great Famine. Their willingness to work in unskilled jobs for lower wages threatened to undermine the employment of Yankee mill girls.[xxii] The old Puritan social order of the region ruptured at its base. In an age of discord, political organizations like the Know-Nothing Party began appearing, garnering widespread support by pandering to anti-immigrant sentiments.[xxiii] The undiscerning eye of the competitive free market was cast upon the region and New Englanders faced a new reality in which their labor was easily replaceable.[xxiv]

Waltham witnessed a large influx of immigrants. By 1850, one quarter of the town population was Irish.[xxv] Nonetheless, the type of industry that would become central to the town and the timing of its arrival diversified the industrial landscape in ways that shielded Waltham from the upheaval occurring elsewhere. In 1854 watchmaker Aaron Dennison opened what would become the largest watch factory in the world on the newly acquired south side of Waltham. His invention—a durable, elegantly manufactured, affordable watch, was revolutionary, and the process by which he intended to produce large numbers of them presaged Henry Ford's assembly-line method of building cars.[xxvi]

Dennison's huge factory along the Charles River was the antithesis of stereotypical New England mill buildings. Equipped with large windows and high ceilings, the factory allowed clean air to pass through, ensuring that fine-tuned watch parts were free of dust while providing ample light for precision manufacturing.[xxvii] A Swedenborgian Christian, Dennison believed deeply in charity, and his workers were treated with a kind of respect previously unheard of in the mill system.

Unfortunately, the precarious financial position of the new venture made this approach fiscally unsound and his partners turned against him.[xxviii] His proclivity for spending large sums of capital on research and development, the generous wages for employees, and the economic recession of 1857 combined to cause his downfall and the Boston Watch Company declared bankruptcy in May of that year.[xxix]

Despite his financial failure, Dennison left behind the apparatus for a world-class watch production system. Appleton Tracy & Company, predecessor to the American Waltham Watch Company, purchased Boston Watch at auction the month it closed.[xxx] Dennison's precedent as owner, and subsequent three-year employment as a foreman for the new company, most likely helped to ensure that the new owners maintained much of his employment ethic.[xxxi] The predominate types of work at the factory often required such specialized training that for the first time in the American Industrial System, the skills of the labor force necessitated that the company owners consider the long-term ramifications of their employment standards before instituting unfair policies.[xxxii]

Though not yet fully established, the rapidly expanding Appleton Tracy & Company insulated Waltham as the next crisis loomed. The Civil War devastated the mill industries, which were dependent on southern cotton, whereas the need for precision military supplies extended to the watch industry.[xxxiii] Though Waltham experienced economic instability, it was spared the extreme economic assault that struck many other mill towns in both wartime and reconstruction.[xxxiv]

When Swinton arrived in Waltham two decades later, he had just discontinued his own personal newspaper, "John Swinton's Paper" after four years of near-continuous struggle to keep it going. That year, he was locked in a battle for a state senate seat in New York—one he would ultimately lose by a small margin.[xxxv] Leaving the tenements of New York behind him, Waltham must have seemed nearly utopian.

The contrast between New York and Waltham makes it difficult to discern what precipitated Swinton's work observing the factory and its employees. He may have had a genuine interest in the Watch Company system. He may have hoped to use the pamphlet as reverse propaganda in the national labor movement. The factory owners may have hired him, believing that a John Swinton piece could keep the strikes occurring elsewhere across America at bay. He may simply have taken the job on contract, in accordance with his press club outburst, a jumping jack tied to a capitalist string.

It is intriguing that his pamphlet is not wholly

uncritical. He clearly documents the disparities in wages between the sexes and he hints that he has concerns about the ways in which the company appears to regulate interactions between male and female employees. But he also identifies early examples of successful union organizing and socialized health benefits, principles that are not enshrined in most of the country today. In an age when factory injuries were frequent and gruesome, his acknowledgement of low mortality rates and absence of child labor at the factory is significant. His discussion of immigration is much less comfortable, but read carefully with knowledge of his other works, his discourse reflects a common sentiment from the time—that immigrant laborers were more likely to be exploited by factory owners than native-born citizens because of their looser ties to the communities where they came to live.

Swinton repeatedly mentions his fondness for Robbins Park, a large, elegant open space constructed by the Watch Company across the street from the factory. He states that the company director, Royal Robbins, knew that the park increased the value of the company's holdings in the neighborhood, but that Robbins also felt "that the chief value of agreeable and wholesome surroundings was in their moral influence upon the workpeople, and that, leaving out of consideration the obligation as well as the delight an employer should feel in providing for his employés the best practical conditions of labor, it is clearly his best interest so to do."

Neither the best interest of the employees nor the value of the land was the motivating reason for the construction of the park. It was designed to limit dust from the surrounding area getting into the mechanisms of the watches. Yet this fact makes Robbins' sentiment even more striking. It demonstrates that the factory made serious efforts to balance the needs of the workers and the company in ways that were mutually beneficial for all parties involved.[xxxvi] This small point illustrates the strange way that even the potential misstatements of Swinton's document do not appear to undermine the striking vision it portrays, of the Waltham Watch Company as an unparalleled institution in American industry at that time.

John Swinton devoted his life to creating a world that would respect the universal human right to safety, dignity, and health. Over half of a century after "A Model Factory in a Model City" was written, American Waltham Watch Company employees had earned sufficient spending money to give rise to one of the first community hospitals in America, a comprehensive public transit system, numerous major technological industries, and one of the most successful Main Street retail centers in American history.[xxxvii]

It would be wholly inappropriate to presume the total success of any endeavor and though entirely unique in the ways that they embraced the Industrial Revolution, Waltham and its foremost employer were not wholly free from the problems inherent to the factory system. Yet Swinton's utopian aspirations and the singularly positive place this piece occupies within his body of writing call into question the frequent imposition of a somewhat pessimistic lens on the world, historical and otherwise.

It is possible that John Swinton came to Waltham to write a 16-page advertisement for the American Waltham Watch Company. But it is also possible that he came to Waltham to write about an instance of something he thought beautiful and could find nowhere else—a model approach upon which he believed other communities could create what he found best here. The ambiguity makes John Swinton's view of Waltham a fascinating, strangely uplifting, and gloriously vexing window into the past.

Laurence A. Green
Waltham, Massachusetts

A MODEL FACTORY IN A MODEL CITY:

A SOCIAL STUDY.

In the State of Massachusetts there is not a lovelier or more attractive town than Waltham, on the Charles River, a few miles west of Boston. Signs of thrift and prosperity are on every hand. Everything looks "well kept." The people you see afoot, or in carriages, or around the houses; the boys and girls on their way to school; the infants in their dainty vehicles—all have a like look. To myself, just from the seething City of New York, the first sight of Waltham was a most enjoyable change.

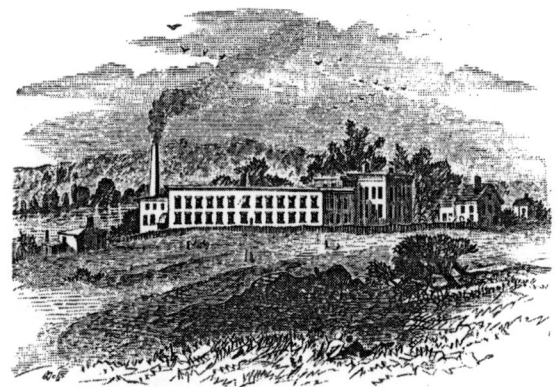

THE WALTHAM FACTORY IN 1853.

A Model Factory

    Driving up a broad avenue, through a picturesque park, I found myself before one of the most remarkable industrial establishments ever built; the largest watch factory in the world, the oldest in the United States, the most perfect in every way, yet devised by human genius—the American Waltham Watch factory. It is a vast series of buildings presenting a frontage of nearly eight hundred feet, and with wings, towers, courts and offices. In front of it is the umbrageous park and behind it the gleaming river. Immediately in the foreground are lawns bordered and decorated with flowers and shrubbery, among which the ancient gardener is at work. It is a superb spectacle, thus to behold this vast hive of free and fair American industry amid scenes which show at once the character and spirit not only of its founders, but also of its thousands of busy operatives of both sexes. When I was told that many of the elegant dwellings I had passed were the homes and property of the workmen in the factory; when I had seen a part of these cheerful workers crossing the lawns on their way to dinner; when I had caught a glimpse of some of them in one of the wings of the establishment; when I had looked at the product of their ingenuity and skill, I became deeply interested, and determined to stay a few days in Waltham, for the purpose of looking, not into the marvelous mechanism of this colossal workshop—all of which is beyond my comprehension—but into the life and ways of the twenty-five hundred men and women who swarm in the halls of this world famous factory.

It is proper to say here that the growth of Waltham has been dependent chiefly upon that of the watch factory, the steady development of which, during the past thirty years has been an unremitting source of welfare to the whole population; and that it is by the resources and disbursements of this factory, and by the industry, intelligence and virtue of its operatives, that the hundreds of pleasant dwellings, of which one gets a bird's eye view from the factory observatory, have been added to the city.

On my own account and by the desire of the courteous President of the Company, I made a thorough observation of the whole factory and all its features, from the engine room, through the numerous departments in which are carried on the delicate and complicated processes of watch manufacturing, involving I was told not far from four thousand distinct mechanical operations; and as I did so, I marveled not more at the automatic machinery which our inventors here put to service, than at the ingenuity and deftness of the men and women who perform such operations as are not within the scope of mechanism. I mingled freely for a whole week with the operatives, whose courtesy and intelligence made it pleasant to ask questions or to converse with them. I visited them at their homes in the evening, and inquired about their work, wages, ways of life and social enjoyments. Still farther, I was assigned quarters in a great boarding house for the gentler sex, established by the Company for those who desire to dwell in it, and where I took my meals thrice a day, with 150 of the young women employed in the watch factory. In short, I made a survey from workshop to domicile, from pay-roll to style of living.

THE CHARACTER OF THE WORKERS.

In the first place, I was struck with the *quality*, so to speak, of the operatives of both sexes. "You won't find a more independent set anywhere in creation," said a townsman of whom I made inquiry. I found the remark to be true. I saw no sign of subservience or slavishness, which as one is apt to look for in a factory. They are respected and self-respecting men and women, shrewd, intelligent, and of excellent demeanor. The men are clad for comfort; and the women, who are of course more tasteful in attire, do not, even in the factory, neglect those personal adornments which are the especial delight of the fair sex. In the faces of the operatives, instead of the pallor which one might expect to see, are health and vigor;

and many of the young women display cheeks as rosy and eyes as bright as rustic school girls; and even after the day's work you will see them tripping along as nimbly as if they had passed the hours in play. While writing these very words, up in my quarters after supper, I hear, above the sounds of the piano, and the noise of the romping, the merry laughter from the groups of demure damsels down below, where parlor, halls and piazza are free for their service.

The heads of the establishment tolerate no tyranny or abuse by any of the foremen of the departments, or by anyone else; and President Fitch himself is an ever open and easily accessible court of appeal to any complainant. As a consequence of such things as are here spoken of, and also of the liberal scale of wages that has always been paid, there has never been a strike in the watch factory since it was established—in the year 1853—a fact that is probably unprecedented in the history of any other branch of industry in the United States. "The factory stands alone in this respect," said a Waltham editor to me, "as well as in respect to the condition of labor within its walls."

AN AMERICAN INSTITUTION.

Another rare feature of this factory is seen in the circumstance that nearly all of its people are Americans by birth. There are few other factories of any kind in the country, about which this can be said. For many years Carroll B. Wright, Edward Atkinson, David B. Wells, and others have been telling of the disappearance from the New England mills of the Yankee girls,- tens of thousands of whom used to be employed there; and they have been telling of the influx from Europe and the British provinces adjacent to this country, of another class who put up with poor pay, hardships, and a kind of living which is certainly not conducive to their own welfare or to that of the community, and which just as certainly lowers the level on which American industry should stand.

ROBBINS PARK

Let these gentlemen visit the Waltham Watch factory, and they will find that though there is not the slightest barrier against the employment of any one on account of race or birth, the workshops are filled by young men and women of the soil, almost wholly of New England lineage—the sons and daughters of the farmers, and towns-people who have given the New England States that character for which they have been so long renowned.

No question of child labor disturbs the watch factory, for the reason that it is not employed there at all. Boys from sixteen to eighteen years old, and girls of about the same age, are put to work at such branch in the factory as may be assigned them, and are advanced in pay as they acquire skill and efficiency. They are apt to stay there till manhood and long after, as children of a State which, not less than Connecticut, is the "land of steady habits;"—in fact, I found middle-aged men, who had been there from ten to twenty years, and elderly operatives whose term of employment dated back to the foundation of the factory.

As with one sex so with the other. The girls are taught in one department or another; but in their case there is always the likelihood that matrimony will, in course of time, take them out of the labor market. The work to which the softer sex are assigned is always of a lighter character and much of it is very dainty and delicate, requiring keen eyes and deft fingers, but neither trying to the mind nor injurious to the body. You often see their workstands adorned with engravings or other fancies; and I found that there was danger of a visitor causing a smile all along the line if he chanced, for example, to have his beaver tilted at one side as he meandered through the departments. I mention such trifling incidents merely as illustrative of the presence here of a spirit wholly different from that crushed and cringing spirit which you often see in other factories. Throughout this great army of systematic operatives, there are order and discipline, both of which are, as they must be, perfect from the time the engines start until they stop. This does not, however, imply the hardships with which these terms are often confounded, and they may not be incompatible with even a casual smile or twinkle, or whisper, or picture on the wall.

The welfare of the workers in the watch factory has conduced, in every way, to the advantage of its owners, and mutual respect has led to mutual benefits. There is here a measure of cooperation such as I have seen nowhere else between employés and employers. They strive to promote each other's interests and only those who are behind the scenes in a great manufacturing establishment can comprehend the extent to which the common prosperity may be thus promoted.

PUBLIC DIGNITARIES.

I have so far spoken in general terms of the character and condition of the work people in the watch factory, but now in the way of illustrative facts, take a few like the following:

The Mayor of Waltham (an incorporated city of 16,000 inhabitants) is an employé of the Watch Company, and at this very time holds office while at his daily work in the factory. I am told that about half of the Aldermen of the city work in the factory, performing their public duties in the evening as the Mayor performs his. There are many other workmen in the factory, who take an active part in the city's affairs. I find also at these benches many capable of exhorting, or leading in prayer, or singing in the choir. This is a novel state of things to me, and I confess that it seemed very curious, when I first passed through the factory, to be introduced to a foreman in one of the departments as Mayor Fisher, and still more so, when, within a few moments, I was introduced to four Aldermen, one deacon, two directors of the public library, the chief of the city fire department, several militia officers, and a member of the brass band belonging to the factory, which gives performances in Robbins Park, and is said to be one of the best bands in the State; all of these dignitaries being factory operatives, drawing their weekly wages; men who feel neither above their places in the workshop nor below their dignity as municipal functionaries. I need not tell how I had reason to believe that there were also Knights of Labor here, plying their trade of watch making,but it is just as well to say that the right of organization is never interfered with by the Company, and could not be.

Still further, I find that quite a number of the workmen, besides owning their houses, are stockholders in the Company, among which are also several of the women, drawing their dividends as regularly as their salary. Such men as I have spoken of are not by any means "tools of the Company," but have their full share of Yankee independence, political and social, and are not the least afraid to show it, when it is called for. You find among the female operatives plenty of accomplished women who, as we say, "move in the best society" of the place, but of whom it were better to say that they *are* the best society in the prosperous city of Waltham.

INTELLECTUAL LABORERS.

"You can't find in any other factory,"said boarding-house keeper Hight to me, "such an intellectual class as these people are here." I found that among those who had been graduated, so to speak, within a few years, there are not a few who have become distinguished in other vocations. Among the examples given me I notice six physicians, two editors, three clergymen, seven lawyers, two artists, one college professor, one veterinary surgeon, and one actress, besides teachers and others in various professions. I had the happiness, while in town, of becoming acquainted with both of the editors, who are of opposite parties in politics, but who agree in speaking with pleasure of their years of life in the watch factory.

It does not seem necessary to say here that such a thing as drunkenness is almost wholly unknown among the men in the watch factory, and so far as they are concerned, there does not appear to be any need of Prohibition, which has been adopted by the people of Waltham under the "local option" law of the State.

A DEPARTMENT AT THE FACTORY.

I have spoken of the boarding-house for female operatives, maintained by the Company, which looks for no profit from it, and there is a like institution for the men, not thus maintained, though the Company, which gave it certain privileges, prescribes that the price of board in it shall be fixed at a low rate. But it must be noticed that it is a privilege, not a requirement, for anyone to board in either of these houses, and it must be also understood that only a very small proportion of the workers in the watch factory live in them. Many, as I have already said, dwell in houses of their own, and the remainder, or the great majority, find such quarters as suit them, with the families of fellow operatives, or in other households of the city. There is, as a matter of course, the utmost freedom for every one in this respect. The advantage that the Company secures to the employés by the two big boarding-houses under its supervision, direct and indirect, is that by this means the prices of board are established for the whole town, so far as concerns the watch factory men and women, at as low rates as are consistent with good living and proper quarters.

THE OPERATIVES.

The precise number of operatives in the watch factory during the week of my visit was 2,471, of whom 1,350 were males and 1,121 females. The majority of the women are about twenty years old, and unmarried, but adding to these such as are of longer service, the average age of the whole body is twenty-six. To be exact about the matter of matrimony, the total number of wives in the factory, most of whom accompany their husbands to work, is 224, or just one-fifth of the whole, thus showing that not fewer than 897 are yet enjoying the bliss of maidenhood. The majority of the men are about thirty years old, but the average age of the entire number, is thirty-two.

The proportion of the males who are married is far greater than that of the females. In truth, the majority of the former are married, as appears by the fact that out of the whole 1,350 just 621 suffer the solitude of bachelordom, and many of these are too young for wedlock. An interesting subject for study is suggested by the comparison just made, but it must be avoided at this time.

I have already spoken of the predominance of operatives who are of American birth, and after tabulating a mass of facts which were procured for me, I find that of the total force only 120, all told, are of foreign birth, not a few of these being natives of the British provinces. All the operatives of both sexes have enjoyed a common school education. The day's work in the watch factory is ten hours, except Saturday, when it is nine, making fifty-nine hours for the week, or one hour less than the time prescribed for youths by the Massachusetts factory law. The women do not work overtime at any season of the year, and it is rarely that the men are ever asked to do so; and on such occasions, of course, extra pay is given. There never was any Sunday work in the watch factory. In midsummer, there is a fortnight's vacation for all hands, and every holiday of the year is observed.

WAGES.

The account books of the watch factory, indicating the pay of all hands for each and every week of the year, were placed at my service. It must be premised that all the work, so far as possible, or perhaps three-quarters of it all, is done by the piece, or, as it is here called, by "the job ;" and it must be further understood that the clause in the "Declaration" of the Knights of Labor which provides that "women shall be paid equally with men for the same work," is rigidly observed. But the variation of earnings in the several departments, or according to the measure of capacity in the operatives, is large.

There are a few men of exceptional skill who earn as high as $4.50 or even $5.00 per day, and I find, in the account of one department, the sum of $5.50 set opposite a man's name; but the average wages of the best-paid men in the twenty-three departments of the factory is $4.00 per day, and of the best-paid women $1.75, though there are female operatives earning as high as $2.60 per day. Taking the whole body of male employés, of every grade and all degrees of competency, the average wages per week are $15.24 ; and taking the female employés in like manner, the average wages are $7.76, or somewhat more than half the average of the men. It must be remembered that these averages include girls and boys of all ages, and beginners of all grades. Furthermore, as regards the average earnings of the women, allowance must be made for the fact that the number

A DEPARTMENT AT THE FACTORY.

of inexperienced operatives of their sex is far greater than that of the other.

The business of watch making, as here practised, is subdivided into very many branches, requiring as many different machines; in fact, I am told that there are no less than 3,746 distinct mechanical operations in the making of a stem-winder, while an ordinary watch requires 150 separate pieces, and many classes of the workers perform only a single simple operation continuously, such as boring a little hole with the needle of a machine, or polishing an almost invisible edge, or making a nice adjustment of some of the minute parts. The earnings of such workers are, of course, less than of those who are engaged in branches that require hard training, rare expertness, or special knowledge. I find that in several branches the average weekly wages for men are not over $11 or $12, while in as many others they run from $16 to $20, or even over; and I find, also, in looking over the rolls, that the earnings of the other sex are largely dependent upon the special character of the work on which they are employed. But I have given enough figures for the reader to form a general judgment upon the whole question; and, in order to compare the statistics of wages here quoted, with those of other industries in Massachusetts, he may consult the reports of Carroll B. Wright and the National Census.

AT THE ADAMS HOUSE.

As already mentioned, I was permitted to stay a week in a boarding-house where one hundred and fifty of the young women, a very few married couples, and a half dozen bachelors boarded. I wanted to see for myself the home life of this portion of the operatives, and I was assigned to a room among the dormitories on the second story, and to a place among other boarders at the table. The house is a large four-story, single-winged wooden structure, with portico and piazza, and surrounded by grass plots. Its whole business is managed, in behalf of the Company, by a janitor and his wife, who procure the supplies, hire the servants, superintend the kitchen, provide the table, and look after the general service. There is a dining hall capable of accommodating the whole body of boarders at once. The bed-rooms are plainly furnished, well lighted, well ventilated, and heated by steam pipes. My room, which is like the others, has papered walls, a large rug on the floor, a table, a washstand, a chest of drawers with looking-glass, an arm-chair, a rocker and an ordinary chair, and a broad bed which is comfortable and clean. At one side is a small closet in which trunks and clothes can be kept. On the walls are a few pictures.

The housekeeper informs me that the young women take care of their own rooms, and keep

A Model Factory

them tidy, adorning them with engravings, knick-knacks, books, growing flowers and pretty trifles. There are two large parlors, open at all hours to every boarder, and there is no restraint upon the freedom, merriment and movements of the inmates. I found the appointments and conveniences of the establishment to be excellent in every respect. I found the table supply to be varied and abundant, or rather superabundant. The bill of fare for the first day may be given here as a fair example of the daily table. The house bell was rung at six o'clock, and in half an hour we were all ready for breakfast, which, too, was ready for us. We had the best of beefsteak, with

THE ADAMS HOUSE.

baked potatoes, boiled eggs, white and brown bread, biscuits, doughnuts and snaps, butter and condiments, coffee and tea. Clean table napkins were beside every plate. At a few minutes after twelve the great rush of the hungry damsels is repeated. For dinner we had soup, scolloped oysters, roast beef and mutton, boiled potatoes, celery and pickles, pudding and pie, with tea, coffee and pitchers of milk. For supper we had cold meats, cheese, various kinds of bread and "fixings," and again coffee, tea or milk. Another day we had poultry at dinner; another morning we had country sausage, besides omelette, and chops, as well as ham, for breakfast; another evening we had canned fruits with our supper. At all the meals throughout the week there were daily variations in the fare. As for the appetites, so far as a stranger could take notice of such a thing, they were somewhat amazing to a man who is unaccustomed to sitting down at table with such an array of Yankee girls.

In the evenings there were lively times all over the house. Bevies of girls were seen everywhere. They sang, they romped, they thrummed the piano, they played games, and a few took side-long glances at the visitor, who gazed with interest upon them. Some of them went out a-visiting or a-shopping. Some went to "sociables," public or private, some attended the grand and dress reception to invited guests in our big parlor; two or three more may have gone to prayer-meeting; a half-dozen struck into a walking match on the highway; some gathered in gossiping groups, while others, I was told, stayed in their rooms to stitch, or to read or write. Soon after nine o'clock they begin to retire, and by ten all is quiet in the house, though the watchman is always there to answer the bell.

THE COST OF LIVING.

The price of board and lodging for women in this establishment (two in a room) is fixed by the Company, which owns it, at three dollars per week, and this rate, as has already been said, influences, if it does not always fix, the terms at other boarding houses in the city for female operatives, though of course when

DINING ROOM IN THE ADAMS HOUSE.

larger quarters are required the prices are increased. The Company is satisfied when the income of the establishment, which is called the Adams House, meets the running expenses.

At the boarding house for men (Shawmut House) where the Company's only authority is in fixing the rates, the price of board for men (two in a room) is four dollars and a half per week, and three dollars for their wives. There are many women and men who take only their meals in these boarding-houses, and secure elsewhere such lodging as may suit them. All these matters are at their own option. It is hard to see why the rougher sex should have to pay one-third more than their sisters for victuals and quarters, but doubtless, after all, the cost of feeding men is greater than that of nourishing women. On Sunday only two meals are given at the various boarding-houses, but in the afternoon an extra grand and generous dinner is provided.

I have had opportunity to see something of the home life of such of the watch factory operatives as own their domiciles or rent houses, many of whom take their co-workers to board. In brief it is the New England home-life, quiet and kindly, in tastefully furnished cottages, most of which are two stories and a half, separated from each other by fences, enclosing grass-plats, trees and flowers. The fare at the table of the families is very much like that of my temporary boarding house, though household economies are apt to be more carefully observed. Some of the operatives who have risen to more than ordinary prosperity live in domiciles more spacious than those of their less successful brethren; and in looking at some of them, as I walked one night with a town officer through the streets, which are bordered with trees, it was hard to believe that they were the homes and property of wage-workers, employed in daily factory labor.

OWNERSHIP OF DOMICILES.

Over one-fourth of all the married workers in the watch factory are owners of the houses in which they live, or to be exact, 190 out of the 729; and the proportion of these house owners has steadily increased year by year. The greater part of them have gained their property out of their earnings within the past ten years, though some of them hold titles dated before that time. The Company has always encouraged them in this course. It has sold to them, at low prices, lots from the body of land which was purchased some time after the establishment of the factory. In many cases it has aided them with loans of money, and otherwise assisted them; and above all else, it has guaranteed them steady employment, whereby they were enabled, not only to clear off all encumbrances, but to enjoy their possessions in safety. There has been no trouble in the practice of this system, and in nearly every instance, all loans have been paid with regularity and promptness. There is also in Waltham, a co-operative loan association, started mainly by workers in the watch factory, which furnishes money to those desiring to build, the amount borrowed being payable in monthly installments. The value of the houses built and owned by these workers, including the ground, ranges from $2,000 to $5,000, and nothing could be more noteworthy than the contrast between them, and the tenement houses of New York, in which myriads of families cluster. Besides the houses referred to, the Company has built many others, and sold them on easy terms to its employés; and it has built yet others which are rented at low rates.

In short, it has been the steady and uniform policy of the managers of the Watch Company to induce every man in the factory to become the owner of his own house, so that, in the language of the prophet, he may "sit under his own vine and fig-tree, with none to molest or make him afraid." While doing this, it has refrained from interfering in the slightest with the spirit of independence which ought to be the pride of every American citizen. The evidences of this fact were given to me by the operatives themselves. As a stranger wholly unknown in Waltham, I sought everywhere, and among all sorts of people,

A Model Factory

including even discharged employés, to discover some slumbering discontent or some adverse criticism upon the ways or workings of the watch factory; but no such thing could be anywhere found by me.

A LOW DEATH RATE.

One of the facts which has surprised me most, in studying the state of things in the watch factory, is the extraordinarily low rate of mortality among the operatives. I find by the carefully kept records of each of the departments that it is below a half of one per cent. per annum. This is, of course, owing partly to the healthfulness of the locality, partly to the absence of child labor from the factory and partly to the excellent sanitary conditions in which the buildings are kept at every season of the year. It is, nevertheless, proof of a wonderful measure of welfare in the lives of the 2,500 workers now under review. It would not be hard to mention factories in which the death rate runs as high as three or four per cent. per annum.

MUTUAL AID.

To secure the advantages of mutual help in case of need, the operatives established the "Watch Factory Mutual Relief Association," the Constitution of which lies before me. It has 1,428 members of both sexes, more than one-half of them being women. Its object is to furnish aid in case of illness. Among other features of the Constitution, it provides for a Visiting Committee whose duty it shall be to render timely assistance to sick members, who are entitled to draw from the treasury the sum of $4. per week. In the event of death $50. is paid for funeral expenses. The dues of members of the Association are twenty-five cents per month, and the Company makes a yearly contribution of $200. to the treasury. The excellent working of the organization is seen in the fact that at this time it has a surplus fund of $1,000.

In explaining matters to me, the Secretary made the curious and surprising statement, which was based on the records, that though the female members are more numerous by one hundred than the males, the latter have always made the bigger call on the funds of the Association. This fact certainly speaks well for the health of the women. At the same time, in view of the lightness of the dues and the amount of relief given, the state of the treasury speaks well for the health of the whole body of watch factory operatives. I commend these significant figures to the study of all members of similar associations everywhere.

METHOD OF DEALING WITH GRIEVANCES.

Even in the celestial spheres, according to the poem of Ralph Waldo Emerson, there are disputations like that which Abdiel held with Uriel about the "being of a line," and in this watch factory also there are occasionally, though rarely, questions in dispute. Any aggrieved person in the factory is invited to state his or her case at any time to President Fitch, who immediately considers it, and it was my fortune to see one grievance terminated in a very prompt and pleasing way. All appeals of individuals are settled with speed and courtesy. If the grievance is on the part of a number of people, the aggrieved appoint a committee to present their case, experts are called in, the foreman of the branch is sent for, and the matter is settled in joint conference of both sides, somewhat after the manner of arbitration. The cases of moment that arise are very few, not more than three or four in a year. All grievances are and always have been settled amicably.

Surely, when we take into account the very large number of work people in the factory, the magnitude of the interests on both sides, and the complicated nature of the questions that must necessarily arise at times in such a business, we must admit that this is a record of honor to all parties. Both the Company and the operatives have proved faithful to all agreements made between them, and the assurance of this came to me in uniform testimony, not only from the managers, but also from the work people with whom I mingled for a week. Mutual confidence is the ground work of successful coöperation.

LEISURE HOURS.

In making the acquaintance of the men of the watch factory, I soon learned of various clubs and other social institutions of the locality. Some of them are members of a club possessing a reading room and a billiard room at which I was entertained. Some of them belong to the Bicycle Club, the Canoe Club, or the Literary Club. There are plays, concerts and dances from time to time; there are performances in the summer months by the factory brass band; there are boat races and there is a Rumford course of lectures in the winter season. Besides, it is but a short and cheap trip, to Boston, and every night parties are on their way to and fro. In brief, there is no lack of social entertainments for the leisure hours of the people. On Sundays the workers if so disposed, can choose any one of the half dozen churches in which are preached the varying dogmas of the old lights and the new lights, from Catholicism to Congregationalism and even to Swedenborgianism.

At first it seemed that the girls were unduly demure, in accordance with the New England tradition of their grandmothers; but I soon had reason to know of their sprightliness and merriment. They walk out

A Model Factory

EAST BROWN STREET

CRESCENT STREET

in the evening without escort, but generally in pairs or groups, and you often hear of their taking trips to Boston or other adjacent cities in the same way. Marriages between operatives in the factory are occasional. I must add that if the men, when you see the whole body of them emerging from the factory as the noon-day bell strikes the dinner hour, have a hearty and stalwart appearance, you do not need to look long to discover in the procession plenty of young women with handsome figures, pretty faces, and the mien of well-poised womanhood. I am told that in the summer season many of them wear white dresses when engaged at their delicate and cleanly work in the factory. Let it here be said, as a finality, that the decorous conduct uniformly observed between the two sexes employed in the watch factory, is a pledge of that moral quality which is more valuable than all else to the individual and to the community.

About the inventions and the machinery of this colossal factory, which constantly surprises you by its novelty, ingenuity, efficiency and beauty, as you walk for hours through one department after another, and from class to class of the workers, all prosecuting separate but mutually dependent branches of the one great industry, I can say nothing that would be useful. About the magnitude of the product of an establishment that has made over three million of watches, and that has for years past turned them out at the rate of 360,000 per year, it is unnecessary to say anything. About the merits of the workmanship, and the quality of the article, and its worth as an exponent of the superiority of American inventive genius, the testimony must be left to the wearers of these three million watches, and to the medals, diplomas and encomiums sent from the great international expositions of the world. All such matters are beyond my purview in making these brief observations upon my study of the industrial and social life of the men and women of the Waltham watch factory in the first week of this month of October, 1887.

This great, remarkable and successful manufacturing establishment is not run by persons

A Model Factory

claiming to be philant[hropis]ts, but by practical and experienced business [men w]ho fully understand the elements and forces w[ith whic]h they work, and know how to put them all to [best] account, with the largest results.

THE DI[VIDEND H]AND.

I had alm[o]st finishe[d my visit] to Waltham before I had the oppo[r]tunity of [seeing] Mr. Robbins, the treasurer and [th]e acknow[ledge]d head of the factory. In the cou[rs]e o[f] a very pl[easan]t conversation with him I a[s]ked [h]im how he ju[stif]ied to his stockholders the large expend[i]ture he m[us]t have made of the Company's money [in] establishing and maintaining the beautiful parks, [la]wns and gardens surrounding the works, in accordance with a policy so different fr[o]m that of most manufacturers. He replied that the Company had no other money half so profitably invested, and that that was justification enough. It paid, he said, in many ways; in the value it added to the Company's other land and cottages, in the stimulus it gave to tasteful building and gardening in the neighborhood, which had in the course of thirty years thus become the most beautiful manufacturing village in the country. All this is greatly to the advantage of the employés, who are now owners of nearly the whole place. But Mr. Robbins thought that the chief value

of agreeable and wholesome surroundings was in
their moral influence upon the workpeople, and that,
leaving out of consideration the obligation as well as
the delight an employer should feel in providing for
his employés the best practical conditions of labor,
it is clearly his best interest so to do. Anything that
tends to lighten the strain of labor upon the mind,
or serves to promote cheerfulness and contentment,
is an economical advantage. In short, Mr. Robbins
claims that he serves his Company best when he
secures at any expense a willing and contented
service from his employés. Nevertheless, Mr. Robbins
will be remembered hereabout not less for his real
regard for all those in his pay than for the enterprise,
the courage, the faith and the persistence in all
times, good and bad, which have during long years
distinguished the conduct of his responsible office.

A Model Factory

Notes to the Introduction

i Lause, Mark A. *The Antebellum Crisis and America's First Bohemians.* Kent, OH: Kent State University Press, 2009. 51.

ii Waters, Robert. *The Career and Conversation of John Swinton, journalist, orator, economist.* Chicago: Charles H. Kerr & Company. 1902. 12-14. For a broader analysis of "Bleeding Kansas" as well as the attendant, relevant issues of the rise of anti-immigrant sentiments in New York and New England in the Antebellum period, within the context of American social and democratic development see: Wilentz, Sean. *The Rise of American Democracy.* New York: W.W. Norton. 2005. 677-688.

iii Lause, Mark A. *The Antebellum Crisis and America's First Bohemians.* Kent, OH: Kent State University Press, 2009. 51. Also; Obituary. "John Swinton Dead." *New York Times.* December 16, 1901.

iv Swinton, John (editor). *Striking for life: labor's side of the labor question.* New York: American Manufacturing Company. 1894. Preface.

v *Ibid.* The particular disappointment by liberals and bohemians in the corporate rise of Lincoln's immediate associates among the radical republicans in the Gilded Age is ever-present in Green, James. *Death in the Haymarket.* New York: Pantheon Books. 2006 where it receives repeated mention and also, in great specificity in Ginger, Ray. *Altgeld's America: The Lincoln Idea versus Changing Realities.* New York: Funk & Wagnall's. 1958.

vi Riis, Jacob A. *How the Other Half Lives.* New York: Penguin Books. 1997 (reprint). Countless academic works have been devoted to this topic, and though perhaps less objective than others, Jacob Riis' classic work, released in 1890, remains the most evocative descriptive account of New York tenement life.

vii Swinton, John. "The New Slave Trade." *John Swinton's Paper,* January 6, 1884. Reprinted in Shapiro, Bruce. *Shaking the Foundations: 200 years of investigative journalism in America.* New York: Thunder's Mouth Press/Nation Books. 2003. 40-45.

viii Obituary. "John Swinton Dead." *New York Times.* December 16, 1901.

ix *Ibid.*

x For Kropotkin, see Avrich, Paul. *Anarchist Portraits.* Princeton: Princeton University Press. 1988. 86., also Waters, Robert. *The Career and Conversation of John Swinton, journalist, orator, economist.* Chicago: Charles H. Kerr & Company. 1902. 49-50. For Goldman see Goldman, Emma (Candace Falk editor), *Emma Goldman, Vol. 1: A Documentary History of the American Years,* Chicago. University of Illinois Press. 2003. 558. For Walt Whitman see: White, William, "Whitman and John Swinton: Some Unpublished Correspondence" *American Literature,* Vol. 39, No. 4 (Jan., 1968), (547-553), Duke University Press., also the quite revealing Anonymous. "Talks of Walt Whitman", *New York Times,* June 1, 1898. For Eugene V. Debs see Debs, Eugene V. (Robert Constantine, editor), *The Letters of Eugene V. Debs,*

Volume I. Chicago. University of Illinois Press, 1990, 103. For Karl Marx, see Swinton, John. Karl Marx: "Interview by John Swinton." *The New York Sun.* No.6. September 6, 1880., also Waters, Robert. *The Career and Conversation of John Swinton, journalist, orator, economist.* Chicago: Charles H. Kerr & Company. 1902. 50.

xi Boyer, Richard O with Herbert M. Morais. *Labor's Untold Story.* New York: United Electrical, Radio, and Machine Workers of America. 1959, 1972.

xii Nelson, Charles A. *Waltham, past, present, and its industries.* Cambridge, Massachusetts: Moses King Publishers. 1882. 18.

xiii Gitelman, Howard M. *Workingmen of Waltham: Mobility in American Urban Industrial Development 1850-1890.* Baltimore: Johns Hopkins University Press. 1974. 2.

xiv *Ibid.*

xv Volume 1, Proprietors' Records, Boston Manufacturing Company, MSS, Baker Library, Harvard University, September 4, 1813. Also, Dalzell, Robert. *Enterprising Elite.* Cambrige, Massachusetts: Harvard University Press. 1987. **26-27, 29.** Dalzell offers a contextual analysis of the Boston Manufacturing Company's organization structure.

xvi *Ibid.*, 42, though his explication is somewhat through negative inference. Boston merchants especially middlemen, were resistant to domestic industrial production or tariffs to support it, but the War of 1812 and the subsequent economic collapse in the United States was met with increased demand for, and a more robust revival of domestic manufacture before commercial enterprise. The market demand and development is indicative of the impact of the war and its attendant commercial hazards.

xvii *Ibid.*, 36

xviii *Ibid.*, 38

xix *Ibid.*, 45 (pp. 38-45 describe the nature of the company's decision to expand)

xx Gitelman, Howard M. *Workingmen of Waltham: Mobility in American Urban Industrial Development 1850-1890.* Baltimore: Johns Hopkins University Press. 1974. 6. It should be noted that a turnout, or early version of a walkout strike, occurred at the Waltham factories in 1820. It is the first example of an industrial labor strike in American history. Little is known about this instance though it receives occasional, brief mention as in Gregg Easterbrook's, *Sonic Boom,* New York: Random House. 2009.

xxi Nelson, Charles A. *Waltham, past, present, and its industries.* Cambridge, Massachusetts: Moses King Publishers. 1882. 137

xxii Dalzell, Robert. *Enterprising Elite.* Cambrige, Massachusetts: Harvard University Press. 1987. 140-41. Also; Wilentz, Sean. *The Rise of American Democracy.* New York: W.W. Norton. 2005. 677-688.

xxiii Wilentz, Sean. *The Rise of American Democracy.* New York: W.W. Norton. 2005. 682.

xxiv Gitelman, Howard M. *Workingmen of Waltham: Mobility in American Urban Industrial Development 1850-1890.* Baltimore: Johns Hopkins University Press. 1974. 40-1. Dalzell makes the valuable summarizing comment regarding the attitudes of many Yankee New Englanders toward the largest immigrant group, "The Irish were not just strangers; they were outsiders." (see Dalzell, 140)

xxv Gitelman, Howard M. *Workingmen of Waltham: Mobility in American Urban Industrial Development 1850-1890.* Baltimore: Johns Hopkins University Press. 1974. 15, 33.

xxvi Ford visited the Waltham Watch Factory in 1910 and it was rumored to have directly influenced the creation of the vaunted Ford Assembly Line. See; Bryan, Ford R. (ed. Sarah Evans), *Henry's Attic.* Wayne State University Press. 2006. 311.

xxvii Gitelman, Howard M. *Workingmen of Waltham: Mobility in American Urban Industrial Development 1850-1890.* Baltimore: Johns Hopkins University Press. 1974. 15, 229.

xxviii Walker, Lenore Mullen. P*iety Corner and the New Church.* MSS. Waltham Public Library. Archives. Waltham, Massachusetts. RW 974.44.

xxix Nelson, Charles A. *Waltham, past, present, and its industries.* Cambridge, Massachusetts: Moses King Publishers. 1882. 135-6. Also; Carosso, Vincent. *The Waltham Watch Company: A Case History,* Bulletin of the Business Historical Society, Vol. 23, No. 4 (Dec., 1949), 165-187 (170), in which Royal E. Robbins, owner of the newly formed watch company is cited as having slashed wages across the factory by 50%. Though this took place in a time of general economic difficulty, it also may suggest something of Dennison's wage policies.

xxx Gitelman, Howard M. *Workingmen of Waltham: Mobility in American Urban Industrial Development 1850-1890.* Baltimore: Johns Hopkins University Press. 1974. 52.

xxxi *Ibid.*, 52. Dennison and Robbins strongly disagreed as to whether the company should manufacture inexpensive watches for the Union Army. Dennison proposed the idea. Robbins disagreed. Robbins fired Dennison and shortly thereafter they company began production of watches for the Union Army, thereby securing the future of the entire company for years to come.

xxxii Gitelman, Howard M. *Workingmen of Waltham: Mobility in American Urban Industrial Development 1850-1890.* Baltimore: Johns Hopkins University Press. 1974. 74-76. It should be noted that in this summarizing portion of his book, Gitelman references Swinton. The preceding material, however, displays a depth and breadth that goes far beyond Swinton's scople. It appears Gitelman has employed Swinton for tone and summary.

xxxiii Gitelman, Howard M. *Workingmen of Waltham: Mobility in American Urban Industrial Development 1850-1890.* Baltimore: Johns Hopkins University Press. 1974. 41.

xxxiv *Ibid*, 41. The impact of the war was not negligible either. The Boston Manufacturing Company was forced to close during the war years and many other town industries dependent on raw materials from the south were hobbled. The counterbalance of the watch company in the latter war years, however, significantly mitigated the effects on the town as a whole.

xxxv Waters, Robert. *The Career and Conversation of John Swinton, journalist, orator, economist.* Chicago: Charles H. Kerr & Company. 1902. 52-53. A curious note in this chapter: Waters states, contrary to Swinton (54), "I am inclined to think [...] he should [...] have tried to find out some means of reconciling labor and capital, employee and employer [...] and made some appeal to the dominant as well as the dominated class.

xxxvi Mannon, Melissa. *Images of America: Waltham.* Charleston, South Carolina: Arcadia Publishing. 1998. 42.

xxxvii Mannon, Melissa. *Images of America: Waltham.* Charleston, South Carolina: Arcadia Publishing. 1998. Carolina: Arcadia Publishing. 1998.

CPSIA information can be obtained at www.ICGtesting.com
Printed in the USA
BVOW011222090712

294124BV00002BA/1/P

9 780982 724620

Edition Copyright © 2012 by Back Pages Publishers
Introduction Copyright © 2012 by Laurence A. Green
All Rights Reserved

No part of this book may be used, reproduced, stored, or transmitted in any manner whatsoever without the written prior consent of the publisher.

ISBN 13: 978-0-9827246-2-0

For information and inquiries, contact:

Back Pages Publishers
a division of Back Pages, Inc.
289 Moody Street
Suite 101
Waltham, Massachusetts

www.backpagesbooks.com

2345678910

Typeset and designed by Mindhue Studio
www.mindhuestudio.com